For The Love

# of Squeekers

by: Brenda J. Shuman

To order additional copies of this book, contact:
Xlibris Corporation
1-888-795-4274
www.Xlibris.com
Orders@Xlibris.com

Dedication

This book was written to remind children to always mind your parents, to share with your brothers and sisters, to be kind and loving to old people and help them out when they need help, to love and have pity on helpless little animals.

Dedicated to my two sons whom I love dearly; the two best sons ever.

I love you both!

Dedicated to my Squeekers

...

a little raccoon I found in a dumpster May 4, 2012, two to three days old, wrapped in a dish towel, stuffed into a zip-lock bag, then another zip-lock bag and tied up in a plastic grocery bag. Temperature in the high nineties.

I raised him on an eye-dropper, then later on a baby bottle. Boy, could he squeek and chatter. He now lives with Kim Wright, a licensed wildlife caretaker until he is ready to be released into the wild. You sure brought love and joy in my life these past weeks, and to know you made it. Good luck little man!

This story is true about this little raccoon. So I decided to write a Once Upon A Time story book for children.

Acknowledgement

A special thanks to Kim Wright in Byron, Georgia; a special lady who takes care of all kinds of animals and turns those born in the wild loose when they are well enough and big enough to take care of themselves.

She does this with money out of her own pocket. She is the lady that is taking care of Squeekers now, until he's able to go out in the wild on his own. Thanks, and God bless you, Kim, and people like you!

Once upon a time there lived in a big old dark forest a family of raccoons. There was PaPa coon whose name was Mr. Kenny James, and everyone called him KJ for short. Momma coon was Ms. Emily, and she had three baby coons. The oldest was Simon, his sister was Sissie, and then the youngest was Squeekers.

It was a beautiful morning, and the sun was just coming up! Kenny James had to get ready for work; you see he went around to all the elderly animals in the forest, and helped them out with whatever they needed done. Maybe rescuing grandkids from danger, doing some shopping, or collecting firewood for winter. Sometimes he would even give them some extra food his family had saved up.

Now Momma was up early fixing breakfast for Papa, Simon, Sissie and Squeekers. She had a busy day ahead of her too; cooking, sewing and gardening. She had completely forgot it was her birthday. All the kids hadn't forgotten, and they were planning something big. After all, Momma Emily was so very special, and such a good wife and momma.

Simon was going to the old farmer's garden, because Mr. Farley always was cleaning his garden, and throwing potatoes, carrots and peas in the edge of the woods. He could wash them, and him, and Sissie could make a pot of soup for Momma as a surprise supper. Sissie wanted to make Momma a cake too for her birthday.

But Squeekers didn't want to help Simon or Sissie. He wanted to do something special all by himself for Momma. He wanted to go fishing at the pond and catch Momma some fish for her birthday. Now Squeekers had been warned by Momma and Papa not to go to the pond by himself. There was a mean old gator named Crocket that lived in that pond. Squeekers would make a great dinner for Crocket. Now Squeekers didn't listen to Momma and Papa but snuck off anyway, and didn't let Simon or Sissie know where he was going.

Well, as Squeekers was sneaking through the woods to the fishing hole, Simon and Sissie were calling and looking for him. Squeekers was getting closer to the pond; just as he got to the edge, he got his hind foot caught in some vines growing around the edge. Crocket was sunning himself on the bank on the other side of the pond. Squeekers couldn't get out of the vine. He started crying and pulling on his foot, but it wouldn't budge. All of a sudden old Crocket saw him and heard him chattering. He was screaming for Momma, but Momma didn't hear him. Old Crocket slid off the bank into the water and headed straight for Squeekers.

Mr. Alton, the wise old owl, heard Squeekers's distressing call for help. He hooted all the little woodland animals up out of the forest to help save Squeekers. There was Trudy and Suzie: two frogs on a lily pad sunning. Here comes Percy the Possum, Rocky the rabbit and Lizzie and Lucky, the two meanest old crows in the woods. All of a sudden all the animals showed up.

who-who
who-who - whoot
whoot - whoot

First Trudy and Suzie swam over to Crocket, hopped on his head and covered his eyes with lily pads so he couldn't see where he was going.

Percy and Rocky started throwing mud balls, and Lizzie and Lucky flew like dive bombers pecking old Crocket all over his back. So while all this was going on, Alton the owl flew down, untangled Squeekers hind foot and set him on higher ground. Everyone shouted for joy. Squeekers was saved!

In the meantime, Momma Emily was down the road visiting a sick friend, and she didn't know the kind of trouble Squeekers was into. Simon and Sissie got Momma's cake fixed and soup done for her surprise birthday supper.

Papa Kenny James was finishing up gathering firewood for the day. He was going to pick Momma a beautiful bunch of wild flowers for her birthday. They were all so excited to surprise Momma.

Squeekers was so ashamed for not minding Momma he just cried. Not only did Old Crocket just miss him, but he didn't get Momma any fish for her birthday. Well, all the animals that helped save Squeekers from Crocket the alligator felt bad for him; so they decided to get Squeekers some fish. Trudy, Suzie, Lizzie, Lucky, Percy, Rocky and Alton tag teamed Crocket, kept him busy while their other friends caught fish.

Squeekers was so happy he invited all his new friends home to Momma's surprise birthday party. They had a big old fish fry, homemade soup and cake for dessert. Squeekers told Momma what happened at the pond and how he learned a very important lesson on how you should always mind your Momma. Momma just gave him a big hug. He promised to never do that again and they all had a wonderful party!

The End

Printed in the United States
by Baker & Taylor Publisher Services